# STORY HOUR

# BY SARA HENDERSON HAY

STORY HOUR

THE STONE AND THE SHELL
(*Pegasus Award*)

THE DELICATE BALANCE
(*Edna St. Vincent Millay Memorial Award*)

THIS, MY LETTER

FIELD OF HONOR
(*Kaleidograph Award*)

# STORY HOUR

Sara Henderson Hay

ILLUSTRATED BY JIM McMULLAN

Garden City, New York

DOUBLEDAY & COMPANY, INC.

*1963*

Thanks are due to the following periodicals in whose pages some of these poems have appeared: *McCalls* (STORY HOUR, © 1959 McCall Corporation, and SYNDICATED COLUMN, © 1961 McCall Corporation), *Saturday Review, The Atlantic Monthly* (JUVENILE COURT, © 1961 The Atlantic Monthly Company), *The Lyric,* and *Voices.*

*For my sister, Willa Hay Godfrey*

# DEDICATION

*To all the luckless suitors who died trying*
*To scale a slope of glass;*
*To poor Rapunzel, in her tower sighing,*
*To Abelard, at Mass;*
*To Dido, on the headlands, hearing the dying*
*Sound of the oarlocks' ring;*
*And little Abishag, into her pillows crying,*
*Warming an old, cold King. . . .\**

* 1st Kings. 1: 1.2.3.

# Contents

# STORY HOUR

# STORY HOUR

He swung the axe, the toppling beanstalk fell.
Hurrah, hurrah for Jack, the self-reliant.
The townsfolk gathered round to wish him well.
Was no one sorry for the murdered Giant?
Did no one, as the news spread far and wide,
Protest the means Jack took to gold and glory:
Guile, trespass, robbery and homicide?
It is not mentioned in the popular story.

Dear child, leave off such queries and suggestions,
And let that gullible innocence prevail
Which, in the Brothers Grimms' and our own time,
Applauds the climber, and ignores the crime.
How requisite to every fairy tale
A round-eyed listener, with no foolish questions.

# THE BUILDERS

I told them a thousand times if I told them once:
Stop fooling around, I said, with straw and sticks;
They won't hold up. You're taking an awful chance.
Brick is the stuff to build with, solid bricks.
You want to be impractical, go ahead.
But just remember, I told them; wait and see,
You're making a big mistake. Awright, I said,
But when the wolf comes, don't come running to me.

The funny thing is, they didn't. There they sat,
One in his crummy yellow shack, and one
Under his roof of twigs, and the wolf ate
Them, hair and hide. Well, what is done is done.
But I'd been willing to help them, all along,
If only they'd once admitted they were wrong.

# JUVENILE COURT

Deep in the oven, where the two had shoved her,
They found the Witch, burned to a crisp, of course.
And when the police had decently removed her,
They questioned the children, who showed no
  remorse.
"She threatened us," said Hansel, "with a kettle
Of boiling water, just because I threw
The cat into the well." Cried little Gretel,
"She fussed because I broke her broom in two,

And said she'd lock up Hansel in a cage
For drawing funny pictures on her fence . . ."
Wherefore the court, considering their age,
And ruling that there seemed some evidence
The pair had acted under provocation,
Released them to their parents, on probation.

# SEQUEL

And there, in the Beast's place, stood a handsome
  Prince!
Dashing and elegant from head to toes.
So they were married, thus the story goes,
And lived thenceforth in great magnificence,
And in the public eye. She christened ships,
Cut ribbons, sponsored Fairs of Arts and Sciences;
He opened Parliament, made speeches, went on
  trips . . .
In short, it was the happiest of alliances.

But watching him glitter, listening to him talk,
Sometimes the Princess grew perversely sad
And thought of the good Beast, who used to walk
Beside her in the garden, and who had
Such gentle eyes, and such a loving arm
To shield her from the briers, and keep her warm.

# THE GOOSEGIRL

Although on silk and eiderdown I lay,
I never had so comfortless a bed.
As for that minstrel, send the fool away
Before I break his lute over his head.
I will not put another silly stitch
In this fine seam for all the castles in Spain.
I wish I'd never seen the meddling witch
Who changed me from a goosegirl to a queen.

Alas, my darling flock—while I lie late,
Who drives you early to your pebbled streams?
Who brings you home at dusk across the drowsy
Meadows, and past the grove where used to wait
A dark-eyed boy who knows some better games
Than Thimble Thimble, or Ring Around the Rosy.

# I REMEMBER MAMA

The trouble is, I never felt secure.
There we were, crammed into that wretched shoe,
Ragged and cold and miserably poor,
And Mama never knowing what to do.
Most of the time we lived on watery stew,
She couldn't even bake a loaf of bread,
And every night she'd thrash us black and blue
And send the snivelling lot of us to bed.

I used to lie awake for hours, and plan
The things I'd do, when I became a man . . .
And this is why I lurk in darkened hallways,
And prowl dim streets and lonely parks, and always
Carry a knife, in case I meet another
Old woman who reminds me of my mother.

# THE PRINCESS

I'll ask for a red rose blossoming in the snow,
A music box hid in a walnut shell;
Nine golden apples on a silver bough,
A mirror that can speak, and cast a spell.
I'll send them East of the moon, and West of the sun,
For a wishing ring made of a dragon's claw . . .
And they will fail, just as the rest have done,
And I can stay at home, with dear Papa.

Oh sometimes in my silken bed I wake
All of a shiver, and my hair on end,
Because again the terrible dream occurred:
What if one of those suitors should come back
With the impossible trophy in his hand,
And I should have to keep my foolish word!

# INTERVIEW

Yes, this is where she lived before she won
The title Miss Glass Slipper of the Year,
And went to the ball and married the king's son.
You're from the local press, and want to hear
About her early life? Young man, sit down.
These are my *own* two daughters; you'll not find
Nicer, more biddable girls in all the town,
And lucky, I tell them, not to be the kind

That Cinderella was, spreading those lies,
Telling those shameless tales about the way
We treated her. Oh, nobody denies
That she was pretty, if you like those curls.
But looks aren't everything, I always say.
Be sweet and natural, I tell my girls,
And Mr. Right will come along, some day.

# THE BAD FAIRY

Of course, the King *did* break his promise to me,
(A habit not uncommon with royal blood)
And failed to honor certain payments due me
For spells and charms around the neighborhood.
Moreover, he forgot about the Queen's
Pricking her finger with the darning needle . . .
But those were not the reasons, by any means,
I stole the sleeping baby from the cradle.

It wasn't revenge I wanted, nor useless gold,
Nor out of spite to make the mother weep;
Nor even to punish the father for his pride—
But a warm, human thing to love and hold
As if it were my own, torn from my side;
As if, almost, I had a soul to keep.

# WINTER'S TALE

I come of a long line of honest workers,
Down-to-earth, thrifty, with a scorn for leisure;
And I've no sympathy to waste on shirkers,
Or those who pass the time in idle pleasure.
Vagrants and profligates deserve their fate—
So why should I be troubled to remember
One shivering vagabond who, last November,
Came begging food and shelter at my gate?

He'd spent the summer fiddling and romancing
While decent folk laid in the winter store—
My house is snug and warm, the cupboard's full;
But evenings, somehow, seem so long and dull.
I wonder what they're like: music, and dancing. . . .
I wish I hadn't turned him from my door.

# THE WORRIER

I can't help being just a bit uneasy . . .
Although he hasn't actually implied
That I've been uncooperative, or lazy,
He's made it clear he isn't satisfied.
I do my best. But how can I compete
With Midas? And there ought to be a law
Against a talking mule like Bricklebrit,
Or millers' daughters, spinning it out of straw.

One golden egg a day, it seems to me,
Of solid, genuine, twenty-four carat stuff,
And laid like clockwork, ought to be enough.
But I've the strangest feeling, like I said,
That things have changed from what they used to be,
And something heavy's hanging over my head.

# THE MARRIAGE

The King and I are more than satisfied;
It's turned out better than we ever hoped.
He's good to her, she made a lovely bride.
And think how we'd have felt, if they'd eloped!
We're quite aware of what his motives were:
He wanted money, and an easy life,
But in the end we had to humor her,
And all she wanted was to be his wife.

As for that fairy tale she likes to tell
About the Frog who scrambled from the well
And gave her back her ball, all dripping wet,
Then turned into a Prince (that's how they met),
We know he's not a Prince—the point is this:
Our poor romantic daughter thinks he is.

## THE GRIEVANCE

Yes, she's a charming girl; we love her dearly.
She's been with us since both of us were small.
One of the family now, or very nearly,
Though actually we're not related at all.
She was a foundling, and she wandered in
One winter's dusk, out of the rain and cold.
She keeps our house as neat as a new pin.
My brothers say she's worth her weight in gold.

But I've a private grudge that rankles yet,
Try as I may to conquer or ignore it—
And sometimes, when I see her sitting there
The old hurt wakens, and I can't forget
That she ate my porridge, and broke my little chair,
And took my bed. I won't forgive her for it.

# THE DRAGON

My cavern floor is cluttered with their bones.
I am full fed and weary, and still they come;
Some of them riding, armed and helmed, and some
Trudging along on foot, with slings and stones.
All one. The pebbles bounce, the sword blades shatter.
The lances bend and splinter on my scales.
Not strength, nor skill, nor witch's charm prevails.
Knight, huntsman, clerk, the miller's son; no matter.

That nubile Princess in the tower yonder
Will have a long long time to wait, I think,
Unless through very boredom I should blunder,
Unless for very surfeit I should blink,
And, dozing, court the stroke whose consequence
Makes of some fool a bridegroom, and a prince.

# THE SLEEPER

*I*

(*She speaks . . .*)

I wish the Prince had left me where he found me,
Wrapped in a rosy trance so charmed and deep
I might have lain a hundred years asleep.
I hate this new and noisy world around me!
The palace hums with sightseers from town,
There's not a quiet spot that I can find.
And, worst of all, he's chopped the brambles down—
The lovely briers I've felt so safe behind.

But if he thinks that with a kiss or two
He'll buy my dearest privacy, or shake me
Out of the cloistered world I've loved so long,
Or tear the pattern of my dream, he's wrong.
Nothing this clumsy trespasser can do
Will ever touch my heart, or really wake me.

# THE SLEEPER

## 2

*(He speaks . . .)*

I used to think that slumbrous look she wore,
The dreaming air, the drowsy-lidded eyes,
Were artless affectation, nothing more.
But now, and far too late, I realize
How sound she sleeps, behind a thorny wall
Of rooted selfishness, whose stubborn strands
I broke through once, to kiss her lips and hands,
And wake her heart, that never woke at all.
I wish I'd gone away that self-same hour,
Before I learned how, like her twining roses,
She bends to her own soft, implacable uses
The pretty tactics that such vines employ,
To hide the poisoned barb beneath the flower,
To cling about, to strangle, to destroy.

# SYNDICATED COLUMN

Dear Worried: Your husband's actions aren't unique,
His jealousy's a typical defense.
He feels inadequate; in consequence,
He broods. (My column, by the way, last week
Covered the subject fully.) I suggest
You reassure him; work a little harder
To build his ego, stimulate his ardor.
Lose a few pounds, and try to look your best.

As for his growing a beard, and dyeing it blue,
Merely a bid for attention; nothing wrong with him.
Stop pestering him about that closet, too.
If he wants to keep it locked, why, go along with him.
Just be the girl he married; don't nag, don't pout.
Cheer up. And let me know how things work out.

# RAPUNZEL

Oh God, let me forget the things he said.
Let me not lie another night awake
Repeating all the promises he made,
Freezing and burning for his faithless sake;
Seeing his face, feeling his hand once more
Loosen my braided hair until it fell
Shining and free; remembering how he swore
A single strand might lift a man from Hell. . . .

I knew that other girls, in Aprils past,
Had leaned, like me, from some old tower's room
And watched him clamber up, hand over fist. . . .
I knew that I was not the first to twist
Her heartstrings to a rope for him to climb.
I might have known I would not be the last.

# THE FLAW

My wife is beautiful beyond compare.
Her cheek is smoother than the rose's heart;
Her hair's spun silk, her lips a work of art,
Moreover, she's as good as she is fair.
Gentle, unselfish, chaste—she's all of them.
And, in addition, she's extremely rich.
The only trouble is, some stupid witch
Has told her that her every word's a gem.

In consequence, we've rubies by the peck,
Rooms full of sapphires, blue as skies down south,
Bushels of emeralds, and the floor's knee-deep
In diamonds, but I don't get any sleep.
And if she doesn't shut her pretty mouth,
One of these days I'm going to wring her neck.

## ONLY SON

I want you all to meet Thomas, my son.
One moment, till I lift my thumb a bit,
Now you can see him better, under it . . .
That's where I keep him. Don't you think I've done
A marvelous job in pruning him so small
Without his feeling any pain at all?
It took, of course, maternal dedication,
A velvet claw, and tireless concentration.

And here he stands, my tiny pride and joy.
We're more like sweethearts than like son and mother;
He'd rather be with me than any other.
He's thirty-seven, but he's still my boy.
He'd sooner die, he says, than hurt or grieve me—
Isn't he darling? And he'll never leave me.

# THE GRANDMOTHER

You wouldn't think they'd let me live alone
Away out here in the woods, so far from town,
Old as I am, and winter coming on . . .
Still, I suppose, they've problems of their own.
They send the child sometimes, when it's not too
    late,
With an extra shawl, and a little basket of food.
I like to watch her skipping through the gate,
Bright as a robin in her pretty red hood.

I get so lonely, at the close of day,
Here by the fire, without a thing to do.
I've even thought of that poor mongrel stray
That skulks around, so miserable and thin.
Next time he scratches, I think I'll let him in,
And give him a warm bed, and a bone or two.

# LOCAL BOY MAKES GOOD

I hear he's changed a lot since he's been grown.
You'd never know him now; but I recall
He used to be so timid and so small
He'd hardly dare to call his soul his own.
I guess we bullied him, but who'd have thought
That he'd be rich and famous, one fine day?
And handsome, into the bargain, so they say.
I don't begrudge him anything he's got,

But all the same, I'd rather like to remind him
That though we're proud of him, and wish him luck,
Here in the poultry yard he left behind him
He'll always be that scrawny little duck,
All bones and pinfeathers and yellow fuzz,
Who couldn't tell you who his father was.

# NEW ENGLAND TRAGEDY

There never was a man with less ambition.
All that he cared about was boats, and nets,
While she was always worrying about debts,
Forever trying to better their condition.
He never seemed to have the slightest notion
That any woman could want more from life
Than what she had, being a trawler's wife,
Stuck in that dingy hovel by the ocean.

It's not surprising that they finally found her
Out where the tide comes pouring over the ledge,
Down on her knees there at the water's edge,
Babbling about some kind of talking fish
Her husband caught, that really wasn't a flounder,
But a Fairy Prince, who was going to grant her a
    wish.

# THE LOST ONES

If you had been older, maybe, or stronger,
Or known what berries could be used for food,
You might, with luck, have lived a little longer,
And finally found your way out of the wood.
But all the paths your stumbling feet have taken
Only contrived the further to confuse you.
Lie down, poor children. Know yourselves forsaken.
Whoever brought you here intended to lose you.

No one will find you, where the light is slanted
Through the thick boughs, except some bright-eyed
    bird
Grown bold because you have not spoken or stirred.
You were the stepchildren whom nobody wanted.
Lost in a darkening world, poor babes, good-night.
Under the drifted leaves sleep sound, sleep tight. . . .

## PHOTOGRAPH ALBUM

This is the one who climbed a hill of glass;
He almost made it, but he slipped and fell.
And this one leapt a ditch of molten brass,
And this one stormed an ogre's citadel.
This one went searching over the rainbow's rim
For a silver apple, and this one sought a flagon
Filled with the Water of Youth up to the brim.
And here is Daddy, standing on the dragon.

And this one, in the locket, with the flower . . . ?
Oh, just a neighbor boy I used to know
Before my father built that silly tower
And all the suitors came. It's rather dim . . .
He moved away, a long long time ago.
Isn't it funny, I still dream of him.

# THE INVESTIGATOR

It's unprovoked and wanton cruelty.
In the first place, the unfortunate mice were blind.
They couldn't have chased her, since they couldn't
  see
Which way to jump. And secondly, what kind
Of woman is she, to take a carving knife
And maim them so? I never saw a more
Pitiful spectacle in all my life
Than those three tails, limp on the bloody floor.

Maybe she likes to hear things run and squeak . . .
But if it's really *mice* she hates like that
She could set traps, or keep a hungry cat.
There's more in this, perhaps, than meets the eye.
Her husband's not been seen since Monday week.
I think I'll stop by the farm and find out why.

# HOUSEWIFE

No wonder she felt submerged, and put upon,
With such a husband, and those swaggering boys
Up every morning at the crack of dawn,
Strutting around and making all that noise,
(Whatever it was *they* had to crow about,
While she was scratching for their daily ration,
Worrying about the nest egg). I've no doubt
She simply reached a point of sheer frustration.

I'll never forget it to my dying day:
Here she came, flying down the street, and squall-
    ing,
"Look out! Look out! Look out! The sky is falling!"
I only hope, before they put her away,
For once in her life, at least, the poor thing knew
Hers was the voice that everyone listened to!

## ONE OF THE SEVEN HAS
## SOMEWHAT TO SAY

Remember how it was before she came—?
The picks and shovels dropped beside the door,
The sink piled high, the meals any old time,
Our jackets where we'd flung them on the floor?
The mud tracked in, the clutter on the shelves,
None of us shaved, or more than halfway clean . . .
Just seven old bachelors, living by ourselves?
Those were the days, if you know what I mean.

She scrubs, she sweeps, she even dusts the ceilings;
She's made us build a tool shed for our stuff.
Dinner's at eight, the table setting's formal.
And if I weren't afraid I'd hurt her feelings
I'd move, until we get her married off,
And things can gradually slip back to normal.

# MESSAGE TO THE VIGILANTES

I'm worried about the boy who minds the sheep—
Oh, not the one in the blue overalls
Who's always sneaking off and going to sleep,
I mean the little nervous one, who calls
For help when nothing's wrong. He isn't fooling.
I think he's genuinely scared to death.
He says he's positive he's heard them howling,
He swears he's seen their footprints on the path. . . .

I know there've been no wolves around for years;
I know that all you men have more to do
Than answer false alarms to soothe his fright . . .
But even so, if anybody hears
The poor child scream again, won't someone go,
Just to be sure that everything's all right?

# THE WITCH

It pleases me to give a man three wishes,
Then trick him into wasting every one.
To set the simpering goosegirl on the throne,
While the true princess weeps among the ashes.
I like to come unbidden to the christening,
Cackling a curse on the young princeling's head,
To slip a toad into the maiden's bed,
To conjure up the briers, the glass slope glistening.

And I am near, oh nearer than you've known.
You cannot shut me in a fairy book.
It was my step you heard, mine and my creatures',
Soft at your heel. And if you lean and look
Long in your mirror, you will see my features
Inextricably mingled with your own.

E24